Marnie's Scavenger Hunt Handbook

Over 50 Extremely Fun and Easy to Run Relationship Building Hunts

Marnie Swedberg

PublishAmerica

Baltimore

ISBN: 1-4137-1751-9
PUBLISHED BY PUBLISHAMERICA, LLLP
www.publishamerica.com
Baltimore

Printed in the United States of America

DEDICATION

To the three musketeers of fun:

Carole Brumley– extremely fun, amazingly balanced.
Nancy Fisher – open heart, open home; friendship facilitator.
Gwynn Conrad – highly competitive, hostess extraordinaire.

It makes me smile just thinking of the laughter we've shared!

ACKNOWLEDGEMENTS

I am so grateful to my family, Dave, Mark, Keren & Tim, for their willingness to share me with friends, known and unknown, both at home and abroad. To borrow Tim's line, "I love you guys way more than you can imagine!"

TABLE OF CONTENTS

SCAVENGER HUNTS
HAVE GROWN UP

Remember those leaf- and ladybug-collection games we played as kids? Well, these days, scavenger hunts remain ready-fun, but have taken on a whole new look.

Corporate team-building hunts go high-tech: giving out instructions on computer disks with directions requiring a global positioning satellite device (GPS), and completion including several complicated steps involving strategy, creativity and teamwork.

City-wide family reunion hunts include players of all ages and require the groups to do such feats of fancy as video-record a team member dancing with a pink flamingo or take a photo of the team with the owner of a yellow PT Cruiser.

Youth groups tap into the mania of mall madness. Birthday party guests hunt for ingredients required to make their own pizzas, parfaits, and pina coladas. Scout Troops turn otherwise ho hum food drives into exciting competitions with lengthy lists, specific time limits, and great prizes.

In these pages you will find ideas from which I have coordinated dozens of scavenger hunts for people of every age range. Whether the hunt-at-hand is targeted toward thrilling a small group of four and five year olds, or challenging a rowdy bunch of 75 adults, scavenging is great sport and every event has its highlights.

With the help of this book, you will be able to select or custom design a scavenger hunt that will meet or exceed your own expectations and insure that your guests have a blast, both personally and interactively.

HOW TO MAKE EVERY EVENT EXCELLENT

Eager to see your group motivated, competitive, and willing to do almost anything to win? It will happen when you set up a truly fun and fair scavenger hunt where honesty is enforced, teamwork is required, and creativity is encouraged. Do your homework and watch your group dive in with delight.

Here is a set of lists from which you can begin to determine which genre of game would best suit your guests and event goals.

AGE
- Toddlers do best with photos-clues and instant feedback.
- Middlers like to work individually in a small area with a short hunt.
- Teens need mixed groups, with adult drivers, and strict consequences if time limits are ignored.
- Adults should be required to use strategy and to feel intense competition.
- Age-mixed teams (i.e.-church picnics or family reunions) may use the adult rules as long as the adults let the kids do the running.

DURATION
- Young children: no more than one clue or one minute per year of age.
- Pre-teens: 45-60 minutes maximum.
- Teens: loosely structured hunts up to four hours.
- Adults: anything from three minutes to four hours.

GROUP SIZE
- Smaller children need to do hunts individually.
- For older groups, divide into teams of 3-10.
- For hunts that require driving, the number in each group should be limited to the number of seat belts in the smallest vehicle you'll be using.

TYPES OF HUNTS
- Search & Seizure: create a straightforward list of items to collect.
- Riddle-Based: plant clues that lead to more clues.
- Do It & Prove It: use Polaroid or digital cameras or video or tape recorders.

LOCATION & LIMITATIONS
– One table
– In a room
– Inside a home or building
– In a yard or park
– Around a certain neighborhood
– Within a mall, plaza, or other enclosed area
– To the homes of team members & friends
– City-wide

SUPPLIES AVAILABLE
- Some hunts require no supplies, some require a few supplies, and others can be quite expensive. For example, the Bigger & Better Hunt costs as little as one penny per team while an elaborate hunt could include limousines, video cameras, and expensive prizes. It's up to you!

PROP POSSIBILITIES
– Identification items such as matching T-shirts, sunglasses, caps, etc.
– Mood music. You might want to play the theme to *Mission Impossible* or *Raiders of the Lost Ark* while teams are reading their challenge sheets.

POST HUNT ACTIVITIES
– At minimum, have an awards presentation and some refreshments.
– For Search & Seizure Hunts, display the items brought in by each team so the others can see.
– For Do It & Prove-It Hunts, allow time for each team to show their work. Hearing the stories behind the scenes is almost as much fun as capturing them!

AWARDS
– Try to do some kind of an awards program–even it's last minute and cheesy.
– For theme hunts, find prizes that match the theme. Examples: for a Valentine's party hunt, the winning team could each get a Hershey's Kiss. After a room-wide coin hunt, the winner could be awarded a coin counter or piggy bank.

RUN 'EM BY THE RULES

Everybody knows that rules are boring. But imagine a football game without rules! Take just two minutes to peruse this list, and you will protect your reputation as a party planner while providing your guests with a guaranteed good time. Even though this chapter comes first, you may want to find your feature hunt and then come back and review the rules that apply.

BUSINESS ETTIQUETTE
– Planner: Anytime your teams need to go into a business where the challenge requires the assistance of an employee, be sure to get the manager's approval in advance. A few managers will refuse to cooperate, but most are more than willing to play along and some even add to the fun.
– Teams: Be polite, courteous and considerate. No cutting in lines or disruptive behavior of any kind.

OPTIONS FOR ENCOURAGING SAFE DRIVING
– As soon as teams are chosen, but before challenge sheets are passed out, have every licensed driver place their licenses in a special team envelope. Seal it and have them place it in the vehicle's glove compartment. Any team whose seal is broken for any reason will get points deducted or be disqualified.

ORDER OF ARRIVAL
– If your hunt requires the teams to go to the same places for clues, be sure to put the lists in different orders so teams arrive at different times to avoid the potential of poor conduct or vehicle racing.

TOGETHERNESS OPTIONS
1. Your team must stay together. Teams who divide and conquer will be penalized or disqualified, or
2. Your team may divide and conquer as long as no less than two of you are together at any given time. Any team with individual members going off on their own will be penalized or disqualified.

EMERGENCIES
– If for any reason you get separated from your team or you, as a team, realize someone is missing–call home base immediately. The party planner will coordinate a connection point. No points will be docked for accidental separation.

RULES FOR EACH HUNT TYPE

SEARCH & SEIZURE HUNTS are probably the most well-known. In these races the individuals or teams are required to find and collect a certain set of items or information.

Rules for a Basic Search & Seizure Hunt
1. The goal is to capture EVERY item off of the challenge sheet.
2. You must be polite and law-abiding.
3. You must return with your items no later than _____ (time).
4. The first team back with all of the items wins.

Rules for a Timed Search & Seizure Hunt
1. The goal is to capture as many items off of the challenge sheet as possible.
2. Each item is worth ___ points.
3. You must be polite and law-abiding.
4. You must return with your items by _____ (time).
5. You will be docked ___ points for every minute you are late.

Rules for a Search & Seizure Info Hunt
1. The goal is to find the correct answers to every challenge.
2. You must be polite and law-abiding.
3. You must return no later than _____ (time).
4. The first team back with all of the correct answers wins.

Rules for a Timed Search & Seizure Info Hunt
1. The goal is to find the correct answers to as many items off of the challenge sheet as possible in the allotted time.
2. Each item is worth ___ points.
3. You must be polite and law-abiding.
4. You must return with your answers by _____ (time).
5. You will be docked ___ points for every minute you are la

RIDDLE-BASED HUNTS

Contrary to popular belief, riddles are completely optional with scavenger hunts. They can definitely add an element of intrigue, but they can also be disastrous. A poorly written clue can actually ruin the party for an entire team who finds itself lost and losing, instead of hustling and hopeful.

Personally, I hate writing riddles, so I'll spare you my feeble attempts and instead recommend the wonderful book *Treasure and Scavenger Hunts* by Gordon Burgett, which is full of riddle-writing tips.

The option I have employed when doing a hunt with riddles is to ask one of my riddle-writing friends to pen some unpredictable poetry for me. I recommend that you find someone who:

– loves to write riddles and clues;
– is well-balanced with the instructions (challenging vs. frustrating); and
– is fun-loving and really talented with a Rhyming Dictionary.

Besides riddles, consider using coded messages. The easiest code to work with is the number/alphabet code (A=1, B=2, etc.). Print out all messages in number code requiring teams to decode each one before progressing. Some planners run their hunts using just global positioning satellite devices (GPS). The units can track a position within 1-12 feet, so the trick is to find a safe place to plant your collection items which can be easily seen by the team but not threatened by the environment or its guests.

One idea is to combine the use of GPS's with written riddles. In this scenario, once the team finds the location (store, home, where ever) using the GPS, they have the ability to solve the riddle on their challenge sheet, which would then allow them to find the item they are to collect at those coordinates.

Two Popular Riddle-Type Hunts

1. A one-sheet list of directional riddles. When the team has solved and followed each riddle, they find the desired object and head home. The first team back wins. Example of a non-rhyming directional riddle: Turn right where a president meets a saint (Washington & St. Vincent).
2. Riddles found one-by-one, each riddle leading to the next. For example:
   Count the number of exterior lights on this church.
   Drive west that many blocks; your next clue is in the birch.

Rules for a Riddle-Based Hunt
1. The goal is to figure out each riddle and to follow each clue until you complete the hunt.
2. You must return no later than _____ (time).
3. If you simply can't figure out one of the clues, you may call home base for help. Your team will receive a deduction, but you may keep playing.
4. You must be polite and law-abiding.
5. The first team to return to base, having solved the entire riddle with the least deductions, wins.

DO IT & PROVE IT HUNTS

These have become really popular in recent years. The teams compete to complete a set of challenges which they prove by bringing back photos from a Polaroid or digital camera, a camcorder or a tape recorder.

These are almost more fun to debrief than to do. Hearing the stories behind the proofs, as each team tries to out-do the others, can be hilarious!

Rules for a Do It & Prove It Hunt
1. The goal is to creatively capture all of the "proofs" listed on the challenge sheet.
2. Each item is worth the point value listed on the challenge sheet.
3. Record ONLY the required challenges so we'll have time to play it back.
4. You must be polite and law-abiding.
5. You must return no later than _____ (time).
6. The team with the most points wins.

Rules for a Timed Do It & Prove It Hunt
1. The goal is to creatively capture as many "proofs" from the challenge sheet as possible within the allotted time.
2. Record ONLY the required challenge so we'll have time to play it back.
3. You must be polite and law-abiding.
4. You must return with your proofs no later than _____ (time).
5. The first team to arrive back to base with the evidence wins.

LET THE HUNTS BEGIN

CHAPTER 1
TABLE-TOP HUNTS

When the party is indoors, due to pre-made plans or last-minute weather complications, a one-table scavenger hunt may be just the thing. The following ideas will provide a starting place from which your creative juices can flow.

Getting to Know You Signature Hunt

Hand out one challenge sheet per table. Each sheet should contain an identical list of several descriptions like those on the following page. The team is to pass the sheet around as many times as it takes for all of the blanks to be filled in with signatures. Players may only sign if their experience matches the description.

There is no limit to the number of times any given player may sign, but the sheet has to pass through the hands of all the other players before any player may sign again.

The winner is the team who completes all the challenges first or the team with the most signatures when the buzzer rings. (Set a time limit before you begin.)

Design your own personalized program or photocopy the following page for a zero-prep, three-minute, game:

GETTING TO KNOW YOU

I own more than 4 pets.	Name them out loud.
I love blue cheese	
I have more than 2 sisters (not in-laws).	Where do they live?
I have been to Disneyland.	When?
I have run in a marathon.	Where?
I am wearing contact lenses.	
I graduated with a 4.0 GPA.	From where?
I am allergic to penicillin.	
I can say a sentence in a foreign language.	Say it.
I own a red car.	What kind?
I had a birthday party this year.	When?
I am wearing a genuine leather belt.	
My nails are professionally manicured.	
I ate at Kentucky Fried Chicken this week.	
I have visited a foreign country this year.	Which one?
I got engaged in the month of December.	Which year?

More description ideas can be found in Chapter 2 under the "Who Are You? General Questions."

Getting to Know You Item Hunt

Similar to the above race, this challenge sheet should include a list of items which your team members must produce from their pockets, purses or apparel.

The team who comes up with everything first–without leaving their table, or the team who comes up with the most items before the buzzer, wins.

Here are some suggestions for things people may have on them…

– 1995 calendar
– handkerchief
– 2000 coin
– photo of family member
– grocery store receipt
– hand lotion
– sunglasses
– stick of gum
– safety pin
– computer diskette
– recipe
– fingernail clipper

A full list of ideas can be found in Chapter 5 in the "Go Get 'Em Hunt.

Magazine Hunt

This Hunt can be done individually or in teams of two or three. In the center of each team arrange a dozen magazines, a pair of scissors, some tape or glue sticks, and a large sheet of poster board.

Hand out a list of required items that each team should find. The team who finds, cuts out, and pastes the most pictures onto their poster-board in the given time wins.

You may choose to set it up as a race: the team who gets them all first wins.

Finally, consider giving a prize for the most pristine or the most organized poster. Some suggested items to have them hunt for include:

- house
- baby
- telephone
- car
- potted plant
- cat
- rose
- flower arrangement
- dog
- angel
- tree
- bride
- wild animal
- family
- desert
- perfume
- clock
- man
- mini-van
- SUV
- motorcycle
- woman
- computer
- cereal

Count 'Em Up Hunt

For this hunt you must divide players into equal teams. Members of each team should sit at a table and appoint a secretary who has a calculator or is quick at math.

Each team will receive a challenge sheet full of number-related questions. The team whose total score is highest wins. (You may want to give a booby prize for the lowest score.)

The numerical challenges could include:

1. Birth state: count 10 points if you were born in this state, 25 points if you were born in any other contiguous state, and 50 points if you were born in Hawaii or Alaska. Add these all together.

2. Write out your Social Security number. Add each digit to get a total. So, 472-95-0001 would be 4+7+2+9+5+1=28. Add everybody's together.

3. Add everybody's shoe size.

4. Add in everybody's age.

5. Add everybody's last (or average) bowling score. Never bowled? Assume you'd get 65.

6. Add in everybody's ring-finger size. No clue? Use 8.

7. Add in everybody's street or P.O. Box number.

8. Using the code: a=1, b=2, c=3, etc., have each player add up the total number value of their own name including letters from their first, middle and last names. Add these all together.

9. Using the code: January=1, February=2, March=3, etc. Have each player add up their own birth month plus as many as they can of the following: the month in which they were engaged, married and welcomed each child into their family. Add these all together.

Bridal Party Blues

This very simple bridal shower hunt taps into the old saying, "Something Borrowed, Something Blue."

Give each player a piece of paper and a pen. The rule is that they have three minutes to identify everything on their person or in their purse or pockets that is either blue in color or borrowed from someone (before they arrived).

The player with the longest list wins. Any item with any blue on it should count, but each item should only count once.

Color Me Purple Hunt

When you are caught off-guard and need an impromptu table game for a large group, this one is always a big hit!

1. Pass out paper and pens to each table.
2. Have each table appoint a secretary.
3 Explain that the teams will have exactly five minutes in which to identify every possible item or feature of the table participants which contains the color "purple" (or blue or black or whatever color you want).
4. Only items written on the sheet at the end of the five minutes will count.
5. Teams receive points for each item on their list. At the end of the hunt, the table with the most points wins.

Scoring Chart:

Any item from a purse or wallet – 1 point each

Article of clothing – 5 points each

Accessory – 10 points each

CHAPTER 2
'ROUND THE ROOM HUNTS

Do you have an active assembly that needs to stay indoors? A hunt in a room can be lots of fun for any age group. We'll start with the easiest room-wide hunts and build according to the level of challenge.

Letter Hunt

For your next mid-party slump, keep this individual-player hunt in mind. Using the name of your party's guest of honor, or the holiday that you are celebrating, have each guest write the letters down the left side of a sheet of paper. All guests should write the same thing.

They need to make their own acrostic by "hunting" for items that start with each letter. As the host, you get to decide which of these three options to use:

1. Allow only things they can see with their eyes as they look around the room.
2. Allow only what they have on their own person or in their own pockets/purse.
3. Allow only memories of things they have personally done that start with each letter.

The goal is to be the first one finished writing down something true for each letter. It quenches curiosity (and extends the game time) to allow the winner to read his list and then to have others add their unique answers.

Easter Egg Hunt

This old favorite can be played in a room, house, yard or playground. It's the same as you remember—hide the eggs (or any individually wrapped items) and let the kids find them!

Coin Hunt

Before your party guests arrive, get four rolls of coins from the bank—one each of pennies, nickels, dimes and quarters.

Hide these coins everywhere you can within one room. Give each player a bag that is sturdy enough not to tear. A quart-size, freezer-quality ziptop bag works well.

Explain to the players that they will have two minutes to hunt and collect as many coins as possible. At the end of that time, they will each be asked to sort their coins into piles of quarters, dimes, nickels and pennies. Prizes may go to the player with the most coins in each category (total of four winners), and the player with the most coins all together or the most value all totaled.

Appropriate prizes would be coin counters or piggy banks—or simply let them all keep the change they found.

Scrambler Hunt

This short hunt is a transition game that can add excitement during a move from one party activity to the next. Before your guests arrive, decide on a clue that has enough letters for each player to have one letter. You can use one-or-more words in your clue, depending on how many guests you expect.

On colored paper, write each letter of the clue in large print. Cut the clue into individual letters and hide each one around the room.

When all the letters are arranged in the proper order, the clue will reveal the next location to go to, the next activity to participate in, or the next prize to collect. Clue examples include: go bowling, eat birthday cake, get gift bags, etc.

When it is time, let the players hunt until they each have one letter. If you end up with a few extra letters, the first ones can go back and find another clue.

Once all the letters have been found, have the group work together to figure out what the clue spells.

Who Are You?

This one has been around forever, but it's still a perfect ice breaker and it can be tweaked to fit almost any theme.

On an 8-1/2 x 11" piece of paper, make a grid of large squares or rectangles. In each section, type or neatly print a personal description and a line for the signature of a person who can honestly claim the description. The goal is to be the first to get a signature in every section.

Depending on the size of your group, you may wish to require that people sign each sheet only once.

The following zero-prep lists will get you started and give you an idea of

what works generally and for a specific theme.

Caution: If one of your descriptions cannot be matched by anyone in the group, it can lead to frustration and/or multiple winners. If you aren't certain each box can be filled, use a time limit to identify a winner.

GAME 1

I am wearing something pink or red.	I have a sister.	I do not like caramel.
My favorite food is pizza.	I like to play the piano.	My hair is naturally blond.
I have an aunt who lives within 10 miles of my home.	I am wearing a ring with a genuine stone in it.	My family owns a mini-van.
I have never been to Disney Land or Disney World.	I have the same size feet as you.	I am wearing toenail polish today.
I own more than three TVs.	I am wearing a heart.	I have brown eyes.

CATEGORICAL

Favorite Food	Mexican	Italian	Chinese	American
Favorite Treat	Jelly Beans	Reeses	Twizzlers	Snickers
Favorite Sport to Play	Golf	Volleyball	Softball	Bowling
Favorite Sport to Watch	Football	Basketball	Baseball	Wrestling
Favorite Store to Shop	Target	Wal-Mart	Sam's	Price Club
Favorite Color	Red	Purple	Blue	Black
Favorite Passtime	Watch TV	Read	Talk on the Phone	Shop
Favorite Holiday	Christmas	Easter	Thanksgiving	My Birthday
Favorite Season	Summer	Spring	Winter	Fall

CHRISTMAS THEME

My tree is already up and decorated.	I have a poinsettia.	I have sent all my Christmas cards out.
I'm done with my Christmas shopping.	My Christmas lights are already up.	We always hang stockings at our house.
I own a pair of Christmas socks.	I participate in a cookie exchange.	We cut our own Christmas tree this year.
I have lit an Advent Candle this year.	I will be traveling away for Christmas.	We traditionally open gifts on Christmas morning.
I have a manger scene on display at home.	I'll be spending Christmas at home this year.	We traditionally open gifts on Christmas Eve.

CHAPTER 3
HUNTS INSIDE A HOME OR BUILDING

Are the grandkids over for the week, it's raining, and they need a fun and physical, yet mess-free activity in the house? Or maybe you need to create an on-premise activity for a large group in a building you have never seen before.

Indoor scavenger hunts can be put together in no time at all, having never seen the facility, if need be. They provide a terrific diversion from an otherwise humdrum day.

One of the most unusual zero-prep hunts I ever coordinated took place in the elegant Fort Garry Hotel in Winnipeg, Canada. Our vans full of shopped-out women arrived in time for a Chinese buffet dinner in the meeting room. After we had relaxed for a while, we divided into five teams for a List Exchange Hunt that lasted two hours and burned off all those supper calories and then some!

The entire hunt was zero-prep, even the prizes: souvenir Canadian Loonies & Toonies ($1 and $2 coins) purchased at the front desk while the gals were out hunting. In this chapter, we'll progress through the hunts from those requiring the least prep-time to the most.

List Exchange Hunt

This three-part, Search & Seizure Hunt is the one we ran in the Fort Garry and requires only a clipboard, two sheets of lined paper and one pen per team.

Part I:

Each team is given ___ minutes to scavenge the public areas of the building to create a Challenge Sheet and a matching Answer Sheet. Inform the teams that they should come up with the most difficult challenges they can think of, while keeping in mind that they may end up with their own Challenge Sheet to complete. (In the end, it's better competition if you make sure they do not get their own).

There are three categories of challenges they may include on their sheets:

1. Require the collection of a no-cost, readily available item from a specific public location within the building. Example: Get a matchbook from the front desk.
2. Require the team to obtain a certain piece of readily available information from a specific source or location. Example: How many guest rooms does this hotel have?
3. Require them to obtain the signature of a person from a particular location. Example: Get the signature of a waitress working in the hotel restaurant.

Have the teams write the challenges on one sheet, numbering each question, and the answers on the other sheet, making sure that the numbers correspond. The answer sheet will be kept by the Hunt Master during Part III.

There are three cautions to review before allowing the teams to leave.
1. **This is a public place**. Be aware that other guests will not all see the humor nor the high-level importance of our project.
2. **Please: no running, shouting, or rude behavior** of any kind!
3. **Be VERY specific** on your Challenge Sheet.

Example 1:
> Instead of, "What kind of soap is used in the main lobby restroom?" Ask specifically, "What brand… or what color… or what scent…etc?" If you aren't specific, the other team will get the point if they attempt an answer, even if it isn't what you meant.

Example 2:
> Do not have people count anything that is not verified in writing by another source. It is just too confusing. If you have them count steps, for example, when the first team counted, did you include the top or bottom steps, or both? If you have them count pictures in a room, do you mean on the walls, carpet, chair upholstery or what? Only ask for numbers that are written down somewhere.

Example 3.
> Do not include challenges whose solution could disappear by the time Part III is in progress. For example: One of our teams asked the bride at the wedding reception in the ballroom if she would mind signing when the other team came around on the hunt. She was more

than willing! However, by the time they got that far, she was no longer available. Make sure that your challenges can stand the test of two hours! Remember: staff members go on break and a room service tray now on the floor outside Room 210 could be picked up by then.

4.   Finally, for every minute your team is late to return from Part I, your team's Part II instructions will be withheld while the other teams get started. Be prompt!

Part II:

When the teams get back from creating their Challenge Sheets, they will need a breather. This would be a great time for a light snack or beverage break and some music or entertainment.

Part III:

This part of the hunt is an all-out race. Expect this to take approximately half the time required for Part I. There is no need to set a deadline as everyone will finish within 10-15 minutes of each other. The winner is the team who completes their Challenge Sheet first.

Judging this hunt is different from most because of how the questions were collected. Be very lenient! The answers for numerical questions will be off anywhere from 0-25 percent. If it's even close, give it to them. Also, some questions lend themselves to trouble. For example, signatures are hard to read. So a question like, "Who painted the portrait between the lobby elevators?" is tough to correct without seeing it for yourself. The question creation team may have it down as "P. Malung" but the answer may come back with the cursive signature deciphered as "R. Nalran." Again, if it might even be right, let it lie. Basically, unless there is something glaringly wrong, the first team to complete the drill is going to be the winner.

One Store Hunts

Chapter 6 covers mall hunts and you can actually do several of the same hunts within the confines of one store, if that's more your speed.

Number Hunt

Doable in any building, this hunt is easy-to-create and generates lots of activity and interaction.

Use the rules for Search & Secure Info Hunts and be sure to have the

answer key ready: the first teams back may have some wrong answers and need to be sent out again.

By the way, some of these questions require teams to count things. I recommended that you avoid this in the List Exchange Hunt above, and here I encourage it. The difference is that in this hunt YOU are personally checking, and double-checking the answers before the race begins. Due to the time you invest, there can be a clear "right" or "wrong" answer.

Here are a bunch of suggestions to get you started.

1. How many exit/entrance doors are there in this building?
2. How many interior doors to rooms are there in this building?
3. How many closet doors are there in this building?
4. How many steps are there inside this building, not including landings?
5. How many fire extinguishers are mounted in unlocked areas in this building?
6. How many vehicles are in the parking lot? (or specify color, SUV's, etc.)
7. How many light-switch plates are there in this building?
8. How many exit signs are there?
9. How many sinks?
10. How many chairs?
11. How many books in the bookcases?
12. How many pianos?
13. How many light fixtures?

Story Hunt

This hunt has two parts—the hunt and the program.

Give each team of three to four players a brown grocery bag and a card upon which is written the title of a well-known story from the world of Disney or the Bible or whatever, depending on the interests of your group.

Explain that each team must do a pantomime of their story using all of the team members. First, though, they are going to do a scavenger hunt. Without opening closets or drawers, the team should hunt around the home/building to find six items which would be useful to them in their skit.

They have 15 minutes total to collect their six props and get ready. Judges will select two winning teams: one for the performance and one for the creativity of the props found and used.

No-Mess-In-the-House Hunt

Even though this hunt takes a few minutes to set up, I love it for kids because it is easy, has them running up, down, and all around, yet it doesn't mess up the house even the tiniest bit. I set out the supplies ahead of time and instruct the kids that all items can be found without opening drawers.

The winner is the first person to complete all challenges in the order given.

As leader, you'll need to adjust the directions to match your home's layout and then make up several hunt sheets, rotating challenges so no two kids are on the exact same track. Rotate freely as long as you keep numbers one and 23 in the same position.

If your house is exactly like mine, you're all set. Otherwise, you may use this master hunt sheet for ideas from which to create your own unique hunt.

1. Go to the living room and find a brown paper lunch bag which is hidden there.
2. Get a safety pin from the counter in the upstairs bathroom.
3. Get a toy animal from the play area.
4. Do five jumping jacks in the front entry area.
5. Get a sandwich baggy from the kitchen counter.
6. Get a square of toilet paper from the basement bathroom.
7. Run up the stairs, two steps at a time.
8. Get a piece of bubble gum from the kitchen. Stand still, chew and chew, until you can blow a bubble.
9. Get a spool of thread from next to the sewing machine in the laundry room.
10. Hop on one foot ten times.
11. Collect a paper napkin from the pantry.
12. Get a color crayon from the play room.
13. Write your name on a drawing slip and put it in the drawing box at the top of the stairs.
14. Put your color crayon back where you got it.
15. Get a toy truck from the master bedroom dresser.
16. On hands and knees, drive the truck from the bedroom to the top of the steps.
17. Take the car to the play room.
18. Find an envelope on the desk in the play room and address it to yourself.
19. Place the car in the envelope and seal it.
20. Run to the living room and do a somersault.

21. Go out the front door and run around the house to the back door.
22. Ring the doorbell and then come in.
23. Find your leader. She is somewhere in the house hiding. The first one to find her wins.

By the way, for number twenty-three, select your hiding place carefully. I once stood in the shower stall for a LONG time before being found.

CHAPTER 4
HUNTS IN A YARD, PARK, OR AT THE BEACH

These hunts occur out-of-doors and can be staged with specifically planted items to collect or done without anyone intentionally hiding anything. Read on!

Nature Hunt

This hunt can be done individually or in teams. Allow them to bring backonly one of each item.

Use a point system to determine a winner, as you can't be 100 percent sure all of the items on your list will be available naturally on the day of your hunt.

Allot a certain amount of time to look and then if teams find everything before the deadline, the first team back wins.

Within this sample list are several items which teams may find littered on the ground. Including these is optional, but if you do, remind the members that they are performing an act of community service by participating in the hunt.

On the following page is a ready-to-copy sample hunt sheet. If you have time, create one that perfectly suits your facility.

LIMIT: FIND ONLY ONE ITEM PER CATEGORY

10 points	rock or pebble
10 points	aluminum can
5 points	green leaf
5 points	evergreen needle
5 points	pine cone
5 points	blade of grass
5 points	dandelion
10 points	acorn
15 points	feather
5 points	twig
15 points	shriveled berry
20 points	plastic utensil
20 points	candy wrapper
20 points	paper cup
15 points	pop or beer bottle
15 points	gum wrapper
15 points	red leaf
25 points	3-leaf clover
25 points	4-leaf clover
25 points	wild mushroom
15 points	clump of moss
15 points	live worm
5 points	smooth stone
25 points	snail
5 points	leaf with pointy edges
5 points	seed
5 points	shiny rock
5 points	piece of wood
50 points	living lady bug

Unnatural Hunt

This one can be as difficult or as easy you want to make it.One idea is to hand out trash bags and disposable gloves and have kids collect ground litter for five minutes, weighing the bags when they return. Be sure to send an adult with each team to eliminate the likelihood of dumpster digging! The team with the heaviest bag wins.

A more elaborate plan would include "planting" unnatural things all over the area for the kids to find. Items could be brand new. Plant several of each item-type and apply the "finders-keepers" rule, but allow hunters to collect only one of each.

Suggestions for planted items include:
– Bottle of nail polish
– Fingernail clipper
– Pocket knife
– Container of lip gloss
– Glue stick
– Box of crayons
– Glitter pens
– Can of soda
– Bag of Gummy Candies
– Sunglasses

More ideas can be found in Chapter 5 in the "Go Get 'Em Hunt".

Staged Yard Hunt

This one is perfect for a backyard party involving children. Keep a list of items you've hidden. You'll want to check it out when everyone thinks they're done and give extra points if anyone can find any of the still-missing items you read off your list. (This way they won't end up ruining your lawn mower!)

Things you can hide in a yard include:

– Beach or tub toys
– Balls of all sizes
– Plastic bugs, animals, army men, etc.

- YoYo's
- Pocket games and puzzles
- Pens, pencils and other school supplies
- Hair accessories

An added bonus with this hunt is that you may place their collections into a decorated bag to send home with them as party favors.

Life of Christ Hunt

This Polaroid hunt may be done in a park, campground, or all around town.

Each team is given a camera, a Bible, and the task of taking eight photos that typify a different stage of the life of Christ. Give them the examples of: birth, baptism, healing ministry, resurrection and let them think of the rest.

The teams should have at least 90 minutes to complete this task and when they come back they should lay out their team photos in chronological order, accurately portraying the order of events in Christ's life.

Prizes may be awarded for the teams who set up the most creative, most realistic and most interesting scenes.

Optional Rule: Each team member must appear in at least one photo or the team will be disqualified.

CHAPTER 5
HUNTS AROUND THE NEIGHBORHOOD

The beauty of these hunts is that the resources are close at hand and the relationships with your neighbors may be benefitted from such an upbeat activity. Just don't do it too often!

Theme Hunt

This is a great hunt that takes zero prep. Simply send the teams out with a time limit and the goal of attaining a certain number of theme-related items.

They may collect only one item per person they visit, but if there are five people in a home or office, they could conceivably get five items from that one stop.

Select one of these themes or devise your own:
- Things that remind you of Christmas (or the holiday you are celebrating)
- Items that are red (or any color you choose)
- Sets of 16 of anything (or the number of years the birthday person is celebrating). Don't worry: they'll come back with q-tips, nails, etc.
- Mostly empty (or hotel size) personal care items
- Keys: any key the person is sure they don't need any more
- Five pieces of cereal – see how many different kinds you can get.
- Socks that don't have mates

Go Get 'Em Hunt

This is your most basic neighborhood hunt involving a list of items to collect from neighbors. No individual home/office may contribute more than three items and items will not be returned.

There are three ways to play:

1. The first team back with everything on the list wins.
2. The team returning before the deadline with the most items wins.
3. The team returning before the deadline with the most points wins.

41

If the following list of items to collect seems unnecessarily long, forgive me! My goal is to provide you with enough ideas for several hunts. Add complexity (i.e. the item "marble" may become "red marble," etc.), and mix and match to your heart's delight.

- dental floss
- marble
- photograph
- 8 track cassette
- phonograph album
- stick of gum in wrapper
- dried flower
- matchbook
- peanut
- stamp of any kind
- key
- dog biscuit
- piece of fabric
- magazine
- nail
- sock with hole
- silk flower
- small potato
- business card
- key
- packet of soy sauce
- toothpick
- comb
- piece of popped corn
- piece of raw spaghetti
- hotel soap
- bookmark
- shoelace
- empty pop can
- popsicle stick
- pen
- empty aspirin bottle

- plastic fork
- cup with jello in it
- yo-yo
- hula hoop
- airplane ticket
- pipe cleaner
- package of garden seeds
- old belt
- recipe card
- pencil
- empty spice container
- paper clip
- crossword puzzle
- sales flyer
- paper towel
- restaurant menu
- bank deposit envelope
- paint color swatch
- travel brochure
- canceled postage stamp
- dead battery
- old calendar
- piece of ribbon
- clipped cartoon
- twist tie
- sandwich baggy
- square toilet paper
- bar of hotel soap
- empty film canister
- piece of bread
- birthday candle
- dry bean
- post it note
- blown up balloon
- golf tee
- blue gum ball
- toy car
- postcard

- lint from dryer
- cash register receipt
- hat
- egg
- used eraser
- styrofoam cup
- plastic toy gun
- paper cup
- paper clip
- unopened junk mail
- piece of bubble gum
- grocery list
- paint brush
- current-year penny
- stuffed animal
- rubber band
- broken shoelace
- bottle of lotion
- lipstick tube
- bottle nail polish
- crayon
- baby diaper (clean)
- safety pin
- paint can
- bobby pin
- plain white envelope
- ketchup or other condiment packet
- jelly bean
- piece of rope
- bottle cap
- raw green bean
- something in Braille
- fingernail file
- old party invitation
- marshmallow
- disposable cup
- candle
- hairbrush
- old tennis shoe

– twist tie
– raw noodle

Holiday Hunt

This plays out exactly as the above hunt except you require holiday-specific items. Below is a basic Christmas hunt list which could easily include the instructions, "You must sing one carol per item you collect from each home."

– red ornament
– Christmas napkin
– pine cone
– snowman decoration
– bell
– piece of tinsel
– Christmas bow
– pine needle
– Christmas wrapping paper
– red apple
– green apple
– chestnut
– Christmas cookie
– Hershey's Kiss
– red or green candle
– Christmas pencil
– Christmas candy
– Christmas card
– Christmas gift tag
– candy cane
– red or green button

Taped Proof Hunt

Each team is given a tape recorder and a nearly-blank tape. At the beginning of the tape should be *Mission Impossible* music and the riddle-like instructions for finding the list of sounds needed to win the hunt.

Be sure each team has a different starting point and that their sound challenges are listed in a different order, so they don't keep running into each other.

Here is a sample verbal riddle to get them started:

"Under the seat in the front of the car,
Your instructions await.
Record each sound as best you can,
Then return, and don't be late!"

The hunt can be set up in one of three ways:
1. As a race where the first team to finish wins.
2. As a timed event with points per project. The team with the most points wins.
3. As a creative effort. The team using the most sounds worked into the most entertaining story wins. (Requires judges.)

Here are some sound byte suggestions to get you rolling:

- dog barking
- police siren
- toilet flushing
- dinner bell
- telephone ringing
- teeth chattering
- instrument playing
- pop can being opened
- timer ringing
- dryer buzzer sounding
- door slamming
- microwave beeping
- feet running up/down steps
- TV or radio noise
- toy piano
- giggling
- sewing machine stitching
- electric can opener
- file drawer shutting
- people singing
- child's popper toy
- cards being shuffled
- sneeze
- garbage disposal
- clock ticking
- door squeaking

You may increase the difficulty of the scenarios for bonus points.

Acts of Service

This hunt wouldn't be appropriate for every neighborhood, but we had a great time doing in it our rural setting and at least one neighborhood of families enjoyed the fun and the free help.

Caution: Since some of these acts of service will be accomplished inside a strangers' home, be sure to have at least one adult with every team.

Instead of collecting items, your teams will be going door-to-door offering services to people in your neighborhood. The first team back with signature proofs of having completed all tasks, or the team to complete the most tasks before the time deadline wins.

When writing your challenge sheet, be sensitive to peoples' need for privacy. Select only acts of service that would be truly useful and non-threatening.

Warn your teams that some people will not be interested in participating, in which case they should say, "Thank you," and run along to the next house.

Here are some ideas we have used:

— wash dishes
— sweep one room or a porch area (b.y.o.broom)
— sweep the front sidewalk
— carry something heavy for the person
— roll up and shake out a rug
— take out the trash
— rake leaves to fill one garbage bag (b.y.o.bag)

Food Shelf Hunt

The next time your group wants to do a food drive for the local food shelf, give this hunt a try. Time permitting, contact the food shelf manager for help in making up a list of items they need. Ask specific questions so you know which items are most and least useful to them. If time gets away from you, however, the following list includes items usually requested by food shelves.

Use a map to divide your area-to-cover into segments so teams don't overlap and visit the same homes twice.

To create more competition, you may want to add points to your challenge sheet: the more the item is needed or the more valuable the item, the higher the points for obtaining it.

In this hunt there are no limits. Teams will receive points for as many items as they can collect (even identical items) from every house they visit. The more the better!

The winning team will have the most points by the established deadline. Or if you have enough time, let the team win who is first to collect at least one of every item on the list, or to reach a certain point level. Here are some items usually requested by food shelves:

- bottled juice
- canned meat: turkey, chicken, tuna, other
- cake/pie mixes
- boxed potatoes
- tea/coffee
- bread
- bagged/boxed noodles
- bagged/boxed rice
- boxed or canned milk
- condiments
- boxed cereal
- canned vegetables
- canned fruit
- spaghetti sauce
- stuffing mix
- flour/sugar
- cans soup
- macaroni & cheese
- peanut butter
- ravioli
- jelly
- hamburger/tuna helper
- oatmeal/Malt-o-Meal
- jello/puddings
- dry package mixes
- baby food
- diapers
- dish soap
- toilet paper
- shampoo/conditioner
- laundry soap
- toothpaste
- deodorant
- paper towels

CHAPTER 6
HUNTS WITHIN A MALL, PLAZA
OR OTHER ENCLOSED AREA

These hunts can be tons of fun as long as everybody obeys the rules of common courtesy for public places. If yours is an unruly bunch, or even just an active bunch of little boys, you might want to stick with a more manageable hunt area or, at minimum, provide an adult per team to keep things in line.

Look 'n Learn Hunt

You'll need to scope out the area before this hunt, collecting appropriate questions and their answers.

Here are bunch of question types to get you started.

How many... flavors of ice cream at Baskin Robbins, shoe stores, drinking fountains, trash cans in the Food Court, stores whose name begins with the letter "T"...?

Collect... 1 free advertising gift, 2 logo-bags from different stores, 3 different kinds of straws, 4 types of disposable eating utensils, 5 business cards, 6 napkins with different logos, 7 coupons from different stores, etc.

Find the answer to certain questions: Which DVD is in the #10 spot on the HMV chart?

How much do things cost? How much does it cost to have a 24-exp, 35 mm, film developed in one hour at K-Mart?

Where can you buy... the cheapest 12 ounces of Coke and how much is it?

Which store... is running the "Buy two/get one free" sale today?

Cheapskate's Hunt

For this mall hunt you will give each team a list of common items to search for around the mall within a certain time limit.

The goal is to find the item on sale for the least expensive price. The team with the lowest total of all prices requested wins.

Be sure to send along pencils with good erasers so they can better their scores as they have opportunity.

Here's a ready-to-go hunt:

CHEAPSKATE HUNT

ITEM	STORE NAME	BEST PRICE
Reese's Peanut Butter Cup, 2 pack		
Toe ring		
Pair of size 8 women's tennis shoes		
8 oz. bottle of Old Spice After Shave		
24 exposure roll of 35 mm film		
8 oz. Tube of Crest toothpaste		
Square package of gift wrap		
Current copy of Family Circle magazine		
Box of Cheerios cereal		
Individual glitter pen		
1 carat diamond ring		
Dictionary		
Cellular Phone		
Roll of transparent tape		
Box of birthday candles		
Small packet of Trident Gum		
Notebook with blank pages, any size		
Desk lamp		
Tweezers		

Store-to-Store Hunt

I've run this one in malls and a downtown, business area. Most people are really terrific, but you'll find a few who are just too busy for fun. Smile, say thanks, and keep goin'!

Ahead of time, scout for free items that can be obtained from the stores or businesses. Start teams at opposite points so that they run on different paths.

Here are some ideas of free items to request:

> Restaurants: take-out menu, napkin, matchbook
> Business/Agencies: business card, promo item, price list, flyer
> Stores: cash register receipt, sale flyer, paint color swatch
> Service Stations: promo item, window rag, free map
> Book Store/Library: bookmark
> Banks: deposit slip
> Post Offices: change of address card
> Arcades: token
> Theaters: ticket stub, empty beverage or popcorn cup

CHAPTER 7
HUNTS TO HOMES OF TEAM MEMBERS
& THEIR FRIENDS

These hunts are relationally rich and they add a personal touch to the collection process. They are only feasible in settings where team members live within a 20 mile radius of home base.

Bigger & Better

This hunt can be done in a neighborhood, but to add lots of laughs, have teams tap into resources available from friends and relatives within driving distance.

Start each team with a penny or something silly. Instruct them to go out and trade up for something bigger and better. They must decide, as a team, if each proposed trade is actually a move up. They can get only one item (or a matching set) at each stop. They must trade one item for another.

Prizes can be for just the biggest (size) and best (most valuable as is) or for additional categories including:

   – Most Amazing
   – Most Difficult to Dispose of
   – Most Disgusting, etc.

One caution with this one: the final items will be big (like couches, cars, satellite dishes, etc.). In the end, you are going to have to get rid of them somehow. Have a plan, or don't do this hunt!

Theme Hunt

The easiest way to run this one is to send the teams out with a limited time to work. They must limit their collections to only one item per place they stop and all items must match the party theme.

Here is a sample green theme illustration from a St. Patrick's Day party.

- green lettuce leaf
- green pen
- green pencil
- green bean
- green key
- green nail polish
- green pea
- green straw
- green napkin
- green cabbage leaf
- green plastic army man
- green glitter
- green marble
- green lima bean
- green plastic toy
- green Lego
- green apple
- green soap
- green lotion
- green pear
- green toothpick
- green button
- green grape
- green paper
- green envelope

Single-Theme Videos

These are super easy to run and can be a hoot to view as a group. It's best done with people you know, as they'll be comfortable enough to have fun.

Each team is allowed to video record only one challenge per home or business. They must gather a total of 12 (or whatever number you choose) video clips.

Example I: **Carols on Film**

The first team back with video proof of 12 different individuals or groups singing just "one line" of a Christmas carol wins. These should be the first line (or a favorite line) from 12 different Christmas carols, one carol per group.

Example II: **Winnie the Pooh**

Capture friends and relatives responding to this question: "We are recording live right now for a video hunt we are on. Would you help us? We just need you to tell us how you would describe the character, Winnie the Pooh, to a visitor from Mars."

The first team back with 12 actual video clip responses wins.

People Hunt I

This is a zero-prep hunt for any group who lives in a friendly community and wants a bigger party! Teams have to actually go to their own homes or the homes or businesses of their friends and convince these people to return to home base to enjoy ice cream sundaes with the group.

The teams get 100 points per person who makes it back to base within the time limit, but NO points for photos, images or representations–just live bodies! You can run this one of two ways:
1. The Hunt, Points, & Ice Cream Sundaes is the whole deal.
2. After Sundaes you can offer an optional concert or other program of entertainment for anyone who wants to stay.

People Hunt II

This hunt requires about five minutes of prep plus the purchase of the cameras. You will need to photocopy the challenge sheet with headings and spaces for pertinent information below as follows:

The easy tasks will be to photograph a person from each of the following age categories:

      – toddler
      – teenager
      – person between 20 and 40
      – person between 41 and 70

    The challenging part of this hunt is that the team has only six photos left on which to capture photos of the youngest and the oldest person they can find. Be sure they write down their actual birth dates and not just the year.

    The team with the very oldest and youngest people captured in photos, assuming they have all four middler photos, will win.

PEOPLE HUNT 2

Age Category	Photo #	Person's Name	Person's Birthdate & Age

People Hunt III

This one probably only works in a small town. Be sure to have some type of optional party planned for these people after the judging is over. Again, offering a make-your-own-sundae buffet line is easy and appreciated by everybody.

The teams should have one hour to call, visit, go get, and/or divide and conquer in mini-teams of at least two.

They should request their guests to arrive at home base at a specific time (one hour from the beginning of the race).

Allow full points for any guest who arrives within five minutes of the deadline and from then on, deduct five points per minute of tardiness.

Teams may have as many people in each point category as they can find but each guest can be counted by only one team in only one category and the first team who approached them is the one who gets the points.

All categories need not be represented. The team with the most points wins.

- 100 points for someone with a real mustache
- 100 points for someone in their bathrobe
- 100 points for someone who has at least 3 children
- 100 points for someone with a tattoo
- 100 points for someone who was born and raised in this area
- 100 points for a child under age 10
- 100 points for someone who is a grandparent
- 250 points for someone wearing bowling shoes & w/a bowling ball
- 250 points for someone in a baseball uniform
- 250 points for someone wearing roller blades
- 500 points for a nurse (licensed RN or LPN) in uniform
- 500 points for the HS quarterback
- 500 points for the grandparent of a team member
- 500 points for a trumpet player with trumpet who will play "Taps"
- 500 points for a school teacher
- 750 points for a pastor
- 750 points for a doctor (a certified doctor in any field)
- 750 points for a business owner
- 750 points for any member of the city council
- 1,000 points for the fire chief
- 1,000 points for the police chief
- 1,000 points for the school superintendent
- 1,000 points for the mayor
- 5,000 points for someone holding at least 2-dozen fresh-baked cookies, bars or brownies (to share)

People Hunt IV

For this one, teams are going to visit the homes and businesses of people they know, camcorder rolling.

Rule: You may only ask for help from someone you knew before the hunt began. While only one challenge per person is allowed, there is no limit to how many challenges per home or business.

The goal is to capture each victim doing the required challenge. This one may be a race (first team to finish wins) or include a varying point scale and a time limit.

Planner: remember to ask for only as many video clips as you will have time to play back when everyone returns to base!

Here are some actions for your teams to acquire on video:

- Someone doing tricks on the monkey bars
- Someone waiving an American flag
- Someone acting like an elephant
- Someone sharpening a pencil
- Someone mopping a floor
- Someone making a basket
- Someone threading a needle
- Someone milking a cow
- Someone combing their own gray hair
- Someone tying on a pair of gym shoes
- Someone popping popcorn
- Someone watching TV
- Someone jumping rope while reciting a rhyme
- Someone standing on their head
- Someone reciting the Lord's Prayer
- Someone using an ATM machine
- Someone walking through a drive-through window lane
- Someone wearing a helmet
- Someone starting a load of laundry
- Someone wrapping a gift
- Someone driving a car
- Someone eating spaghetti
- Someone cleaning a toilet

CHAPTER 8
CITY-WIDE HUNTS

When you have all sorts of time and plenty of drivers, this is the way to go! Most groups use volunteers' mini-vans or SUVs. Some go all out and hire limos or borrow motor homes. Whatever you do, it will be fun.

Be sure to review the general rules especially the one regarding driving precautions before you embark on this type of a hunt. Also, be very clear about the necessity of arriving back to base before the appointed time, or your party could drag on endlessly.

Finally, with the advent of cell phones, it is easy to provide a contact to home base in case a group gets lost or loses a member.

Have fun!

Create Your Own Hunt

In this game, teams may spend no money nor promise to return any items. Within these rules, they will be judged on how well their collected items match the following broad descriptions. They may collect only one item from any individual person.

This contest is relative so the burden falls on your judges who should complete this phrase when judging items, "Which of these is the most...?"

Bring back something very...

- beautiful
- ugly
- unusual
- common
- colorful
- drab
- large
- small
- reasonable
- unreasonable
- expensive
- cheap
- cheerful
- depressing
- comfortable
- painful
- delicious
- unappetizing
- cold
- hot

Restaurant Race

This is a super-savvy, low-investment hunt that should take about an hour. Use the Search & Secure Hunt Rules.

Each team is assigned a starting point located exactly ___ minutes away from home base in opposite directions. (You choose an "equal distance" that is reasonable in your setting.)

The hunt involves collecting one FREE item from as many different restaurants as possible within the time limit. Proof of compliance will be the logos on the items.

Explain that only two members of a team may go into any restaurant together. (While they are in one establishment, two other members can go into another, but don't take the whole team into any individual place.)

Explain that if they see something in the lobby, like a basket of matchbooks or coupons, they should simply take one and leave without bothering anyone. If not, they will need to wait their turn and then politely request anything that they could take with them that has the restaurant logo on it and explain that "…it's for a scavenger hunt we are on."

Before the teams leave, go over a beefed-up version of vehicle safety. Due to the original drive-time required to get to their starting point, this hunt lends itself to the temptation of extreme speeding at the outset. Increase the consequence of having their envelope's seal broken to "immediate disqualification." You want them to abide by every law and to maneuver through parking lots with care during this hunt.

Finally, in order to make those first travel minutes enjoyable, require that the teams use the ride out to create a Team Name and Theme Song, which will be performed after the hunt. EVERYBODY has to participate in the theme song or the team will be disqualified.

Around Town Item Hunt

An extremely easy option, this hunt can work with no prep except to photocopy the lists. (If you do, be sure to start each team on a different item and have them go in order from there, so they don't cross paths.)

You can go with a straight-out race or else your list can be super-long and you can attach points to each item for a "who can get the most points before the time-limit" race.

A small sack (used for nails) from a hardware store
A discarded cash register receipt from a grocery store
A disposable cup with a company logo on it
A free, promotional pen
A business card
An empty shoe box
A free bookmark
A window sticker from the fire department
A free doggie biscuit
A free insurance promotional item
A free promotional item from a police officer

More suggestions were listed in Chapters 5 and 6.

Back Around the Town

A backwards hunt goes over big and you can almost use the exact list as given above. This time, however, instead of having teams collect the above items, you collect them and then they must return them to the appropriate places.

Be sure that everything has a store label on it or is somehow traceable back to it's original location.

The first team to return all the items to their proper homes and return to home base wins. Two ways to insure compliance are...

1. As you are collecting items, ask the person in charge if you could leave some tokens or tickets with them (one per team). When a team comes in to return an item, the clerk should give them the proof token. The first team back with all of their tokens wins.
2. Send along a sheet of paper. Require each team to collect the signature and phone number of the person with whom they left the returned item.

Around Town Info Hunt

This one takes more prep-work, but it's worth it. Be very specific with your instructions and be sure to collect the correct answers before beginning. Remember, the bigger the city, the more specific you'll need to be with the clues.

Teams may write their answers on the back. Here is a pre-made hunt for

you to either photocopy or use for ideas. Remember to stagger starting points!

What is the year on the cornerstone of the public library?
How much does it cost to wash and vacuum your car at _____?
What are the collection hours for out-of-town mail pick-up at the Post Office?
How big is the biggest pizza you can order from _____?
Whose gravestone is dead ahead when you enter the _____ Cemetery?
How much is a Peanut Buster Parfait this week at the DQ?
What pastor's name(s) are on the _____ church sign?
What color are the swing-seats at _____ Park?
Count the number of exterior doors on the _____ Church.
What is the highest apartment number at _____?
How many total wash machines are in the public area of the laundromat?
How much does the least expensive Kids Meal cost at _____?
What are the service times posted on the _____ Church sign?
How many cookies in a full-size package of Keebler's Chips Ahoy?
How many bird feeders are there at _____?
How much does the "One Month Unlimited Tanning" package sell for right now at _____?
How many calories and fat grams in a Subway Club sandwich

Photo Hunt
This one requires either Polaroid or digital cameras for each team. If using digital, be sure to have the capability to quickly download and display the photos on a big screen as everybody will want to see them!

The sky is the limit with a digital, but a Polaroid camera usually only allows 10 shots–so require eight to win. Either assign a driver/photographer or insist that team members take turns playing photographer.

Items they will need to shoot could include:

– team and team car under a time and temperature sign
– team posing with a Wal-Mart greeter
– team in front of a sign with the numbers 1, 3 and 5 on it
– team peeking around a building with only heads showing
– team standing with a stuffed bear
– team lying on backs on the ground in a circle with their heads together
– team surrounding a gravestone (could be a specific one)

- team drinking a can of soda using individual straws
- team posing on playground equipment
- team making a phone call on a decorative phone
- team jumping in the air at the same time
- team on a fire truck
- team sitting on a sidewalk with one member per cement square
- team posing by a road sign with flashing lights
- team standing (clothed) in a bathtub
- team posing with a car salesman
- team standing in front of a statue or mannequin
- team surrounding a grocery cart with one member in it
- team posing with a pet at a pet store
- team on a bus
- team washing someone's patio window
- team member in the back seat of a police car

Backwards Photo Hunt

This Riddle Hunt requires quite a bit of running around in advance. Instead of giving the clues out in riddles, you will recruit accomplices at each location who will be giving out photographs. As soon as the team is given a photo-clue, they will rush to that location to receive their next clue, until they receive a photo of home base. The first team back wins.

Teams who get lost may call in for clues, but each clue costs 10 minutes or whatever you think is appropriate. (This ten minutes is added to the time the team arrives back. If another team returns before the end of this penalty period, the penalized team loses their first place standing.)

Of course, you would never give this list out to your teams, but so you have some idea of clue positioning, here are a couple of ideas to get you going:

- photo of a small restaurant or storefront (like Joe's Hardware). Have them keep the next clue at the check-out.
- photo of a duty officer at the police station. He'll have the next clue.
- photo of the librarian. She'll have the next clue.
- photo of a church. The pastor has the next clue.
- photo of a school. The office has the next clue.

Bible Story Video Hunt

Provide each team with a Bible, a camcorder and a time limit. Each team must select three (or however many you want) Bible stories to enact on film. Each story should be shot at a different location and should last no longer than three minutes. The winning team will be the one who gets the very best skit including the name and reference of the story, a panoramic view of an appropriate setting, all team members (remember to take turns being photographer), and the most creative presentation.

An alternative is to pass out a set of envelopes each containing one Bible story. The teams may only open one at a time. This is more challenging as they cannot choose their own stories, plan ahead or collect props as they go.

Opposites Attract Hunt

Make up a list of objectives as in any normal hunt. Use the lists found through out this book for ideas. This time, however, the team's job is to figure out something that would be the opposite of the challenge and then to go and do or collect that.

Expect a wide variety of results. For example, during a Search & Seizure Hunt requesting the opposite of a black hat, you might get anything from a white hat to a white sock. For a nail, you could expect hammers, straight pins and anything in between.

Judging this as a Do It & Prove It Hunt is harder, but fun! If you ask for the photo of the opposite of a drinking fountain, don't be surprised to get a picture of a pop machine, a urinal, or a beautiful water fountain.

Scavenge for Signatures

This one is pretty easy to write but not so easy to complete. For a zero-prep hunt, go listless requiring teams to get as many signatures as they can from people in one category of life. For example: owners of Ford vehicles, people walking dogs, etc. Be sure to have them get the signature, the printed version of the signature, and the type of... car, dog, etc.

For a straight-out signature hunt, here are some challenges to consider:

Someone with recently manicured fingernails
Someone wearing bright pink
Someone with a child who is graduating this year
Someone who owns a PT Cruiser

Someone who has been to Hawaii in the past two years
Someone who is six years old
Someone who has a grandchild who is six years old
Someone who has a dog who is sixyears old
Someone whose house has a whirlpool
Someone who golfs under 80
Someone walking a dog
Someone in uniform (any kind)
Someone who plays the accordion
Someone who works for a daycare
Someone who has been at a wedding within the past month
Someone who has received a shot (of any kind) within the past month
Someone whose been to the grocery store today
Someone who has mowed (or shoveled) today

The Make-A-Day-of-It Hunt

This team-building hunt can take four to five hours. Have the final destination be a hang-out place like a beach or bowling alley. That way, if some teams finish in three hours and others take all five, they will have entertainment while waiting.

There are basically four rules for this one:

1. Teams may divide and conquer as long as they stay in groups of two or more.
2. You may only use the original video camera—no dubbing tapes!
3. When the challenge calls for the entire team, that is what it means. You will have to recruit a camera man for these shots.
4. You MAY NOT return to base until you have completed every challenge.

Again with this hunt, you will want to help the judges by providing categories and ribbons within each category. Use a system similar to the one described in Chapter 9.

In the end, the team with the most points wins.

Ideas are limitless with this much time, but here are some general concepts to work with:

1. Video record four team members individually telling one joke each, for a total of four funny jokes. Jokes must be clean (no swearing, sexual content/ innuendo or crudeness). You might have to visit the library for ideas, but points will be awarded for humorous punch lines and great presentations.

2. On video, interview at least four toddlers regarding monkeys in zoos. Each interview must take place at a different location, with a different team member running the interview, and last between 20 and 60 seconds. Points will be awarded for how well the interviewer evokes an initial response and helps the interviewee along.

3. Take intermittent video clips of team members making and decorating a cake. You may not purchase a pre-made cake nor enlist the assistance of any person outside of your group. Points will be awarded for completion, decorating skills, and transporting the cake to the meeting point without hurting the decorations.

4. Figure out one food that no one in your group has ever eaten before. Find it, eat it, and video record each team member giving a verbal or facial reaction. Points will be awarded for creativity and humor.

5. Video record a team-member petting a live farm animal. Points will be awarded for the rarity of the animal filmed.

6. Video your entire team in a tent playing Patty Cake. Points will be awarded for the clarity of the words and the unity of the rhythm.

7. Video record each team member beside a large statue or mannequin of their choosing. No two team members may use the same statue. Points will be awarded for how well the team member explains the likeness they see between themself and the object.

8. Video record a 30-second commercial including all team members. Points will be awarded for the stupidity of the item being sold and the desire factor generated by the commercial.

9. Video the entire team at once, each holding a puppy. Points will be awarded for how many different types of puppies your team can hold with a

maximum of one puppy per team member. More points will be awarded for live vs. stuffed.

10. Video team members taking their turn doing the hula hoop. Points awarded for participation and total team hooping duration. Extra points if someone on your team is captured on video doing a 10 second neck, arm or leg move.

11. Visit a campground or hotel and video a team member conducting a 60 second interview with a traveler who is explaining how far s/he has come to be here. Points will be awarded for the distance from which the interviewee came.

12. Video record a team member in a big boat. Points will be awarded for size of the boat – bigger is better!

Nonsense Hunt

This hunt combines a little of everything and is fun because of its stupidity. In a whimsical fashion, require teams to do a variety of different tasks in any order and to end up at a central location. The first team there with everything done wins.

Here are some ideas of what a non-sense hunt could require. BEWARE: this is not a photocopy-ready hunt. You need to decide which type of hunt to have and then use ideas that fit.

– sing one song for the cashier at 7-11: get a signature
– find a 1972 penny
– look up the word "spectacle" and write out the definition
– go to _____ (restaurant) and ask for an olive on a stick
– have each team member do a different exercise (jumping jacks, push-ups, etc.) in front of a bank teller & get her signature
– look for (and write down the location of) a turkey
– under the influence of helium, have a team member ask for directions to the –park from a stranger. Get a signature that you did it.
– have the whole team do the Macarena near the McDonalds entrance; get a witness' signature
– find and bring back a beanie baby
– write down the phone number for the city morgue

- have your team's picture taken in a photo booth
- make a cross from twigs and anything you can find
- find the cheapest fish you can and bring it back alive
- convince someone to give you something of value
- make a s'more and bring it back with you
- find the owner of a corvette and get a signature
- visit a stranger's open house and ask for a napkin to take with you
- write a poem using every team member's name
- go to the laundromat; place everyone's socks in a dryer; get a signature for proof; put socks back on and leave
- wash someone's car window and get a signature

CHAPTER 9
TEAM BUILDING HUNT TIPS

Team Building Events are a bit more complex, as they must involve strategic thinking, teamwork and creativity. However, many of the hunts in this book can be adapted to these requirements by using the concept that follows.

Two critical factors:

1. Find judges who are respected by the contestants.
2. Clearly define the rules, points, and judging criteria before you begin.

Designate four categories like:

>   Most Predictable
>   Most Humorous
>   Most Creative
>   Most Unexpected

And ribbons within each category:

>   1st place – 500 points
>   2nd place –250 points
>   All Others –100 points

Each photo or object will be given only one ribbon in one category. The team with the most points wins. Just for fun, consider dubbing teams, "Most Creative Team," etc.

Happy Hunting!

ADDITIONAL RESOURCES

In writing this handbook, I limited my recommendations to hunts that I have personally planned, participated in, or seen done by groups in my association. I know for a fact that all of the hunts in this book have been, and can be, done successfully.

But my brain and, more importantly, the Internet, contains limitless additional hunt resources. Instead of including unproved hunt ideas in this resource, I chose to include a list of links to sites that have inspired me. A few offer a resource for sale, but most of these provide scavenger hunt planning services for groups who don't want the hassle of organizing their own party. By simply reading the examples they give in their promotional text, you may find that ideas are triggered in your already-clicking cranium.

I must apologize that by the time this book reaches your hands some of the following links may be non-functional. Such is the nature of the Internet. To find more, use your favorite search engine to look up "Scavenger Hunt." You will be given over 10,000 links from which to find ideas.

http://www.scaventures.com
http://www.drclue.com
http://www.team-building-idea.com/team-hunt.html
http://www.passporter.com/articles/hunts.htm
http://www.teambuildinginc.com/article_treasurehunt.htm
http://www.thepartyworks.com/party-planning/scavenger-hunts/
http://www.thepumpkinshell.com/

Disclaimer: I have no affiliation with any of these organizations and cannot vouch for the feasibility of any of their suggestions.

Printed in the United States
2386SLVS00001B/24

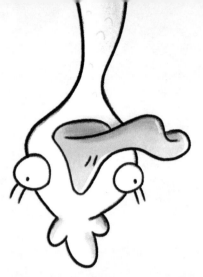

Greetings! My name is Matthew Gallman and I am a cartoonist from Chicago, IL. I made this book when I lived in Savannah, GA and studied at the Savannah College of Art and Design (SCAD) in my senior year.

I grew up reading newspaper cartoons, and in middle and high school I spent my time drawing comic strips for the local paper. I've always been a humor writer and I really enjoy writing comics and books that make people laugh.

I really hope you enjoyed this book, and if you did, keep on the look out for more books that I'll hopefully be making soon.

Step 4

**Add the
finishing details.**

Step 5

**Erase those
unneeded lines.**

Done!

**That duck is
ready to color!**

How to draw the duck

Follow the five steps and draw with a normal pencil where the red lines are
and erase where the blue lines are. Then you can color with colored pencil,
marker, or watercolor!

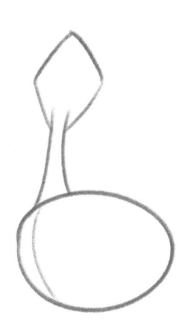

Step 1

Simple shapes for the
head, neck, and body.

Step 2

Add shapes for the
wings, eyes, bill, and hair.

Step 3

Start adding details
for the bill, tail, and legs.

Invite a duck to dinner,
and the night won't go as planned.
Since ducks don't know their manners,
things might get out of hand.

But give that duck another chance
because she's a beginner.
One way or another,
that duck will eat her dinner.

When those ducks realize
that what they did was bad,
they'll hang their heads down low
beginning to feel sad.

"If you ducks clean up your mess
of all the food and dirt,
and if you behave yourselves,
you may stay for dessert."

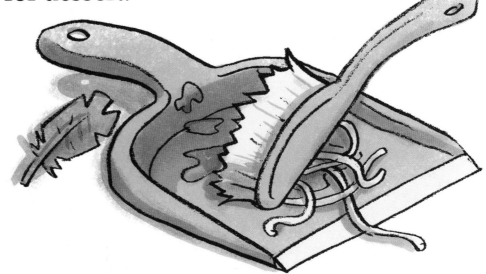

If those ducks continue
to play and run about,
then mother might go crazy,
so you'll have to shout...

"Settle down, you crazy ducks!
You stop it right now!
If you don't start behaving
my mom will have a cow!"

Invite those ducks to dinner,
and they'll fly around and quack.
They'll knock over mother's things;
her flower vase will crack.

They'll squish the squash, snap the peas,
crack the corn, and cut the cheese.
They'll act very foolish
and do anything they wish.

Invite a duck to dinner
and the chaos will begin
when she opens up the door
to let her duck-friends in.

If you think you didn't like
the muddy mess before,
you sure wouldn't want to see
the new mess on the floor.

Invite a duck to dinner.
You'll have red sauce on the walls
when she steps in spaghetti
and starts juggling meatballs.

Invite a duck to dinner,
and she'll fly up in the air,
then make herself a nest
and lay an egg in grandma's hair.

Invite a duck to dinner
and before she has been fed,
that duck will fill her stomach
with potato chips and bread.

She won't be considerate;
she'll scoop and bite and dip.
That double-dipping duck
will always double-dip her chip.

After she's done swimming,
that duck will want to dry.
She'll use sister's scarf
because it is nearby.

When she dries her wings,
the duck feathers will fly.
They'll get into the salad
and in the pumpkin pie.

Invite a duck to dinner
and she'll startle the group
by jumping into mother's pot
and swimming in the soup.

Invite a duck to dinner
and when she sits in her chair,
she'll ignore grandpa's handshake
and rudely sit and stare.

She doesn't know her manners
so she won't sit up straight.
With elbows on the table,
she'll drum on her plate.

Invite a duck to dinner
and when she walks through the door,
she won't wipe her feet
and will leave mud on the floor.

This book belongs to:

duck

I INVITE A DUCK TO DINNER

By: Matthew Gallman

CHICAGO SW. CHRISTIAN SCHOOL
Tinley Park Elementary
17171 South 84th Avenue
Tinley Park, IL 60477

3TINP00220564V

E GAL
4/16
4.99

Invite a duck to dinner was printed by CreateSpace:
an Amazon company in 2016, and distibuted by Amazon.

Invite a duck to dinner was written and illustrated by
Matthew Gallman in 2016. It was created in Savannah, GA
at the Savannah College of Art and Design.

Printed in the USA
Charleston, SC
2016

Special thanks to the assistance of Ahmad Rashad Doucet
and Erica Smith.

www.matthewgallman.com
www.facebook.com/gallmancartoons

CreateSpace ISBN

ISBN-13:
978-1530417629

ISBN-10:
1530417627

DATE DUE

For more books, comics, and illustrations visit www.matthewgallman.com